Hamad Bin Khalifa University Press
P O Box 5825
Doha, Qatar

www.hbkupress.com

First published in Arabic by Hamad Bin Khalifa University Press, 2022.
Translation Copyright © Hamad Bin Khalifa University Press.

All rights reserved.

No part of this publication may be reproduced or transmitted in any form or by any means, electronic or mechanical, including photocopying, recording, or any information storage or retrieval system, without prior permission in writing from the publishers.

No responsibility for loss caused to any individual or organization acting on or refraining from action as a result of the material in this publication can be accepted by HBKU Press or the author.

First English edition, 2022

Hamad Bin Khalifa University Press

ISBN: 9789927155949

Printed in Doha-Qatar.

---

**Qatar National Library Cataloging-in-Publication (CIP)**

Ahmadi, Amina, author.

The world of colors / by Amina Ahmadi ; illustrations by Inna Ogando ; translated by Ghenwa Yehia. First English edition. – Doha, Qatar : Hamad Bin Khalifa University Press, 2022.

  pages ; cm

ISBN 978-992-715-594-9

1. Colors -- Juvenile fiction.  2. Children's stories, English.  3. Picture books.  I. Ogando, Inna, illustrator.  II. Yehia, Ghenwa, translator.  III. Title.

PZ7.1. A36 2022
820.8008 – dc 23                                                                202228353754

# The World of Colors

By Amina Ahmadi

Illustrations by Inna Ogando
Translated by Ghenwa Yehia

In a room packed with toys, Amna has the best time full of fun and imaginative adventures.

She plays with her dolls and dresses them up.

She also builds cities, complete with bridges and towers, using her blocks.

One morning, Amna's mother surprised her with a box, beautifully wrapped with a white ribbon on top.

Amna was very excited, but she was also a bit confused. It wasn't her birthday, or a special occasion. So why was her mother giving her a gift? "A new experience is waiting for you inside this box," said her mother with a smile.

With her heart pounding, Amna eagerly opened the gift to see what was inside.
A set of watercolor paints!

Amna already had sets of colored pencils and crayons,

but she had never tried her hand at painting with watercolors before!

Inside the box were twelve vibrant colors and a long, rounded brush. Amna's mother brought a small cup of water while Amna prepared her sketchbook.

"You must dip the tip of the paintbrush into the water before dipping it into the paint," explained her mother as she gently guided her hand.

Amna was ecstatic to learn a new skill but didn't know which pretty color to choose from first.

Amna looked closely at the colors and contemplated what she could paint.
A field of multicolored roses?
A bright row of houses?
Or maybe some unique patterns?

She decided to start with her favorite color: blue. She dipped her paintbrush in water and then in the paint, just as her mother had taught her.
But when the paintbrush touched the paper, something strange happened!

In the blink of an eye, Amna found herself inside the very drop of water that had been mixed with the blue paint.

She had been transported to another world full of colors!

Amna found herself standing on top of a colored hill, surrounded...
...Light and dark colors...
...Faded and sharp colors...
...Transparent and opaque colors...

Amna pressed her hands against the walls of her water drop to move around and explore. She rolled back and forth until she rolled all the way down the hill and fell into a blue pool!

"Hello, Amna," said a strange voice. "Welcome to the world of colors!"
Amna was amazed. "Who are you?" she asked.
"I'm Cyan, and over there are my friends Magenta and Yellow," Cyan replied.

Amna turned around, fascinated by the wonderful shades and ripples of colors.
"Where did you come from?" she asked in awe.
"How did you get here?"
"We've always been here!" Cyan replied. "We're the colors in nature, in rocks, stones, minerals, plants and flowers."

"All the colors you find in your paints come from pigments that are extracted from nature," Cyan continued explaining to an awestruck Amna.

"That's right!" chimed in Magenta. "And when you dipped your brush in water and then in your color palette, you made us come alive!"

"Painters make us bloom between water and paper," said Yellow brightly.

"Tell me more about colors!" said Amna. "We are not constant," Cyan replied. "Whenever the brush moves and the amount of water changes, so do we. From light to dark, or from opaque to transparent."

"Think about all of the wonderful shades of yellow you see in nature," continued Yellow. "We are all the same, but different."

Amna nodded her head in agreement. "You're right. The yellow of a lemon is different from the yellow of a banana or a sunflower."

The three colors nodded, pleased at Amna's perceptiveness.

"You see, we are the three primary colors," Cyan explained as they moved along. "And when we mix and fuse, we can generate countless other colors."

Amna watched as both Cyan and Yellow crossed the same path, and a broad green meadow lay flat before them!

"What do you think of that refreshing green that Yellow and I made, Amna?" Cyan said with a big smile.

Amna clapped in delight as Cyan continued his show, moving towards Magenta until they flowed together in a mesmerizing dance that caused purple waves to crash around them.

"Many people think that my cousin red is a primary color," explained Magenta, "but mixing red with blue doesn't always give such a beautiful purple! That's why I have been nominated a primary color."

Magenta began to splash colored drops towards Yellow, who was at the top of a high mountain. When the two primary colors met, a bright orange waterfall began to cascade down towards them.
"Look, Amna!" shouted Yellow. "We made orange! Isn't it so bright and fun?"
Amna reached out to touch the orange waterfall spray, laughing as she said, "It really is!"

Amna's mind raced with questions.
"How many new colors can I make with my paints? Dozens, maybe hundreds!"

Lost in a world of new possibilities, she didn't realize that the water droplet that had taken her to this new place was drying up around her, until suddenly it was gone!
And in the blink of an eye, she found herself back in her room, with her paints laid out in front of her.

She began to draw the magical world of colors on her paper. And every time she dipped her water-soaked brush in the colors and then swept it across the blank paper, she was once again on a magical adventure.